English Army and Navy Lists

Compiled During the
American Revolutionary War
by
Ansbach-Bayreuth Lieutenant Johann Ernst Prechtel

Edited by
Bruce E. Burgoyne

HERITAGE BOOKS
2007

HERITAGE BOOKS

AN IMPRINT OF HERITAGE BOOKS, INC.

Books, CDs, and more—Worldwide

For our listing of thousands of titles see our website
at
www.HeritageBooks.com

Published 2007 by
HERITAGE BOOKS, INC.
Publishing Division
65 East Main Street
Westminster, Maryland 21157-5026

International Standard Book Number: 978-0-7884-4148-5

Following are the English and "Hessian" Regiments, which served in the colonies during the American Revolutionary War, and the names of their officers.

English Regiments

Staff of the Army in America under the Command of Sir Guy Carleton

General and Commander-in-Chief, the right honorable
Sir Guy Carleton
Lieutenant Generals,
The right honorable
Charles Earl Cornwallis
James Robertson
Major Generals, honorable
William Phillips

John Campbell
Alexander Leslie
Brigadier Generals
Charles O'Hara
John Leland
Francis McLean
William Dalrymple
James Paterson
Samuel Birch
Thomas Stirling
Aide-de-camp to the Commander-in-Chief
Major William Crosby
Major John Lloyd
Major [Emanuel Anshelm von] Wilmowsky, of the Hesse-Cassel Mirbach Regiment
Lord Clinton
Lieutenant Colonel Watson
Captain St. George
Lord Dalrymple
Lieutenant Colonel Bruce
Lord Chewton
Captain Keppel

Lists

Secretary to the Commander-in-Chief
John Smith, Esq/
Assistant Secretaries
Captain Phillips
Captain Russul
Aides-de-Camp to the Right Honorable Lieutenant General Charles Earl Cornwallis
Captain Broderick
Lieutenant Haldane
Captain Ross
Lieutenant Money
Ensign Fitzroy
Aide-de-Camp to Major General Leslie
Captain Skelly
Aide-de-Camp to Major General Campbell
Captin Adenbrooke
Deputy Adjutant Generals
Major Despard
Major Magenzie
Major Delancey
Captain Barry

Assistant Deputy Adjutant Generals
Lieutenant Bibby
Cornet Stapleton
Quartermaster General
Brigadier General Dalrymple
Deputy Quartermaster General
Lieutenant Colonel Schedriffe
Assistant Deputy Quartermaster Generals
Major Handfield
Captain Vallancy
Captain Campbell
Lieutenant Rankin
Lieutenant Durnford
Lieutenant Gilfillon
Lieutenant Pardon
Lieutenant Armstrong
Ensign Newart
Bridge Master
Captain Lawton
Assistant Bridge Master
Captain Abson

2

Lists

Majors of Brigade
Major Moncrieffe
Captain Small
Captain Scott
Captain Studholm
Captain Bensonlm
Captain Lewis
Captain Brabason
Captain Campbell
Captain Cameronl
Captain Williams
Captain Baillies
Captain Collins
Captain Boyd
Lieutenant Mezner
Lieutenant Wyngard
Engineers at Halifax
Captain Spry
Captain D'Aubant
At Penobscot
Captain Hartcup
At Florida
Captain Durnfort
Command Engineers at
South Carolina
Major Moncreiffe
Lieutenant Haldane

Lieutenant Durnfort
Command Engineers
At New York
Major Robertson
Captain Mercer
Lieutenant Parker
Lieutenant Fyer
On the Expedition with
General Leslie
Lieutenant Suther-
land
On the Expedition with
Brigadier General
Arnold
Lieutenant Stratton
Major and Director of
the Guides
Samuel Holland,
Esq.
Commissary General of
Stores and Provisions\
Daniel Wier, Esq.
De4puty Commissary
General
Major Morison
At Southward
Brindley, Esq, of
New York

3

Lists

Assistant Commissary
Generals - At Halifax
   Crawford
At New York
   Butler
On the Expedition with
General Leslie
   Hecht
At Charleston
Townsend, Esq.
At Long Island
   Johnson, Esq.
Inspector and Superin-
tendent of HisMajesty's
Provision's Train
   Clark, Esq.
Commissary of Muster
   Pitscher, Esq.
Deputy Commissaries
Of Muster
   Porter
   Webb
   Gent
Commissaries of Pris-
oners
   Winslow, Esq.
   Loring, Esq.
   Caloner, Esq.

   Walter
Deputy Judge Advo-
cate
   Payne
   Adye
Assistant Judge Ad-
vocates
   Captain Blucke
   Ensign Wood
Deputy Paymaster
General
   Thomas, Esq.
Barracks Master
General
   Major Crosbie
Barracks Master for
New York
   Lieutenant Brown-
ing
Acting Barracks Master
For New York Island
   Lieutenant Grant
Barracks Master at
Georgia
   Captain Moore
At St. Augustine
   Scheriffe

4

Lists

At Pensacola
Captain Rainsford
At Charleston
Captain Mahon
At Bermuda
Lieutenant Blan-
dell
At Island St. John
Nesbit, Esq.
At Halifax
Morden, Esq.
At Penobscot
Ensign M. Lauch-
lin
At Long Island
Lieutenant Baddely
Acting
Captain Howison
Lieutenant Stuart
At Staten Island
Bonnel, Esq.
Town Major for New
York
Lieutenant Hewet-
son
Town Adjutant at New
York
Jordan

Provost Marshal
Cunningham
Deputy Provost
Marshal
Fiva

Lists

Civil Branch
Of Ordnance

Principal Commissary
and Paymaster to the
Royal Artillery in North
America
   Grant, Esq.
Storekeeper
   Stephens, Esq.
Commissary of Horse
at New York
   Scott, Esq.
Clerks of Store at New
York
   Man
   Mead
   Fraser
   Sterns
Conductors of Stores
at New York
   Sibnclair
   Clopper
   Philips
   Arstin, Jr.
   Plant
   Mead, Jr.
   Ried

   Stephens
   Enssow
   West
   Hardy
Assisant Commissaries
of Horse at New York
   Curtis
   Fraser
Conductors of Horse at
New York
   Tomlinson
   Stockes
   Clout
   Thomson
   Wipple
   Davidfson
   McGuyer
   Brown
   Williams
Clerks in the Pay Office
   Grosvenor
   Gordon
Conductors of Stores at
Nova Scotia
   Brown
   Deas

Commissary of Artillery in South Carolina
- Wichy, Esq.

Conductors of Stores at South Carolina
- King
- Hale
- Ferguson
- Von Aschendelft
- Philips

Assistant Commissary of Horse at South Carolina
- Forbes

Conductor of Horse at South Carolina
- Oram

Clerk of Stores at Georgia
- McDonald

Conductor of Stores at Georgia
- Fraser

Clerk of Ordnance Survey with General Leslie
- Uhthof

Conductor of Stores With General Leslie
- French

7

Staff of the General Hospital

Superintendent of all the Hospitals
Nooth
Physicians
Wald at New York
Roberts, Acting Chief Surgeon at New York
Hayes, at South Carolina
Surgeons
Malet, Purveyor at New York
Grand, Field Inspector
Foster, South Carolina
Field, New York
Hope, New York
Beaumont, New York
Auchinlek, New York
Westhill, South Carolina

Schmid, on the Expedition with General Arnold
Loring, with General Leslie
Apothecaries
Croker, at New York
Payne, at New York
Proker, at New York
Mace, at South Carolina
Edwards, Georgia
Bisop, New York
Haddeston, South Carolina
Watson, New York
Deputy Purveyor
Morris, South Carolina
Established Mates
Turner, New York
Harris, New York
Cormick, New York
Edmonstone, West Indies

Drammond, New York
Kerr, Light Infantry
Atkinson, on expedition
Muir, with the Grenadiers
Kendrik, South Carolina
Edie, Quartermaster at New York
Reid, New York
Young, a prisoner
Smith, South Carolina
West, New York
Lindsey, South Carolina
Ebden, with the 84th Regiment
And in New York
Hatcher
Merrik
Wright, Sr.
Cormick
Auchmaty
Browne

Broker
Boggs
G. Drummond
And in South Carolina
Jenkins
Teare
Supernummerary Mates
Sinclair
In New York
Ball
Germmill
Hicks
Stevenson
Mckay
Bakler
Bayeux
Morgan
Carter
In South Carolina
Boyd
Campbell
McLeod
Allen
Douce
Kincaid
Lind
Hinyeston

Wright, Jr.
Steel
Grenadiers
    Leith
Light Infantry
    F.B. Campbell
    Gamble
    Skinner
Expedition
    Bell
    Murray
Dep. Captains
    Moore

Lists

Brigade of Royal Artillery

Colonel Pattison
Lieutenant Colonel
Cleaveland
Major Martin
Captains
Farrington
William Johnston
Huddleston
Wood
Thomas Johnston
Brady
Fraille
Stewart
Williams
Lemoine
Scott
Adye
Tiffin
Captains Lieutenant
Lawson
Faye
Ford
Measure
Wilson
Hare

Douglas
Abson
1st Lieutenants
Abot
McLeod
Colleton
Wilson
Duvernette
Desbrisay
Robets
O'Hara
Trotter
Smith
Luye
Cockburne
Thomas R. Charleton
Haddern
William Charleton
Rogers
Bowater
Scott
Horndon
D'Arcy

11

2nd Lieutenants
- Scott
- Lawson
- Frasier
- King
- Pattison

Chaplain
- Badger

Adjutant
- Reid

Quartermaster
- Ford

Surgeons
- Destaleur
- Morris

Mates
- Almond
- Buckler

1st Battalion of Guards

Brigadier General O'Hara

Captains and Lieut-Colonels
- Howard
- Leland
- Lincoln
- Thomas
- Horton
- Stuart
- Hall

Lieutenants and Captains
- Hoorneck
- Parker
- Boscawen
- Vockrane [sic]
- Maynard
- Jones
- Dundas
- Maitland

Chaplain
- Cooke

Adjutant
- Wilson

Quartermaster
- Furnial

Surgeon
- Rush

Mate
- Hopkins

Lists

2nd Battalion Of Guards

Captains and Lieutenant Colonels
Gordon
Guidickens
Pennington
Lovelace
Schulz
Watson
Hamilton
Lieutenants and Captains
Swannton
Beauklerk
St. George
Schulz
Goodricke
Watkins
Richardson
Christie
Mathew
Eid
Chaplain
Cooke
Adjutant
Colqulroun

Quartermaster
Hill
Mates
Gordon
Kier

17th Regiment of Light Dragoons

Colonel Preston
Lieutenant Colonel
Birch
Major Delancey
Captains
Archdale
Talbot
Needham
Baggot
Lieutenant Colonel
Bradshaw
Lieutenants
Nettles
Kerr
Cook
Pattishal
Hussey

Lists

Cornets
Oflevie
Stapleton
Searle
Tucker
Jones
Paterson
Clair
Black
Chaplain
Becker
Adjutant
Jones
Surgeon
Johnson
Agents
Cox, Mair, and Cox

**Seventh Regiment of
Royal Fusiliers**

Colonel Prescott
Lieutenant Colonel
Clarke
Major Crosbie
Captains
Newmarsh
Baillie

Layard
Helyar
Home
Despard
Shuttleworth
Selwyn
Lieutenants
Burrowes
Edmund Sutherland
Cliffe
Ford
Walker
Brown
L'Estrange
Twysden
Grant
Prideaux
Symes
James Shuttleworth
Garforth
Lane
Helyar
Harling
Jones
Philipps
Marshall
Rawstone

14

Edmund Shuttles-
worth
  Azlek
  Regnett
Chaplain
  Walker
Adjutant
  Wood
Quartermaster
  Taylor
Surgeon
  Hazelton
Agents
  Ross and Gray\

9th Regiment of Foot

  Colonel Legonier
  Lieutenant Colonel
Hill
  Major Forbes
Captains
  Money
  Dobbyn
  Shelden
  Baillie
  Gray
  Annesey

  Swettenham
  McLean
Captain Lieutenan
  Smith
Lieutenants
  Vincent
  Fife
  Prince
  McNeil
  McMurray
  Keymis
  Richardson
  Peraro
  Hoey
  Fish
  Piercy
Ensigns
  Wadell
  Gwynn
  Wormsley
  Fielding
  Spener
  Orchard
  Dean
  Leslie
Chaplain
  Wood

Lists

Adjutant
  Fielding
Quartermaster
  Murray
Surgeon
  Scaley
Agents
  Cox, Mair, and Cox

**Sixteenth Regiment
Of Foot**

Colonel Robertson
Lieutenant Colonel
Dikson
  Major Gardiner
Captains
  Boyde
  Conner
  Jones
  Arbutnoth
  Forester
  Barker
  Smith
  Murray
Captain Lieutenatt
  Usher

Lieutenants
  Carrique
  Home
  Carrol
  Sproule
  Skinner
  Barwell
  Rankin
  Heyes
  Lindegrin
  Gordon
  Hazelson
  Allan
Ensigns
  Broke
  Finnagan
  Fenwick
  Spence
  Newland
  Lucas
  Bowen
  Lord Monagu
Chaplain
  Edwards
Adjutant
  Hamilton
Quartermaster
  Lowe

Surgeon
  Thomas
Agents
  Cox, Mair, and Cox

**Seventeenth Regiment
Of Foot**

  Colonel Monckton
  Lieutenant Colonel
Johnson
  Major Armstrong
Captains
  Darby
  Cayton
  Hooke
  Weich
  Nodes
  Magra
  Brereton
  Scott
  Saymour
Captain Lieutenant
  Cuppidge
Lieutenants
  Armstrong
  Shairpe
  Miles

Ashe
Amiel
Willaims
Haymann
Harding
Carey
Wetherall
Fraser
Simpson
Mawhood
Ensigns
  Desbrisay
  Jackson
  Corser
  Luscastor
  Hamilton
  Amiel
  Stovin
Chaplain
  Lloyd
Adjutant
  Hamilton
Quarterrmaster
  Herzog
Surgeon
  Horne
Agents
  Hugh,   Esq.   And

Hundfard, Esq.

Twentieth Regiment Of Foot

Colonel Parker
Lieutenant Colonel
Lind
Major de Strang-
ways
Captains
Rollinson
Winchester
Power
Farquhar
Wemyss
Culliford
Stanley
Captain Lieutenant
Banks
Lieutenants
Gaskill
Gilbert
Crofts
West
Dobson
O'Meara
Norman

Loyd
Terriano
Charlton
Batemann
More
Ensigns
Parr
Connel
Svory
Wolfeley
Jones
Grier
Cooper
Bolton
Mau
Gasgoyne
Chaplain
Baker
Quartermaster
Holmes
Surgeon
Cahill
Agents
Cox, Mair,
And Cox

Twenty-First Regiment of Foot

Colonel Makay
Lieutenant Colonel
Hamilton
Major Forester
Captains
  Disney
  Farmer
  Brodie
  Kirkman
  Lindsay
  Lovell
  Petrie
  Poynton
  Starkie
1st Lieutenants
  Hepburne
  Douglas
  Burnet
  Hobart
  Noble
  Cox
  Alcock
  Schlagel
  Innes

Blakwook
Ross
Dugliesh
Lewis
2nd Lieutenants
  Ball
  Darrah
  Lindsay
  Leith
  Brown
  Peddie
  Massey
  Douglas
  Aspinal
  Fletscher
Chaplain
  Browne
Adjutant
  Kirkman
Quartermaster
  Lauder
Surgeon
  Pemberton
Agents
  Messrs. Ross and
Gray

Twenty-Second Regiment of Foot

Colonel Gage
Lieutenant Colonel Yorke
Major Erskine

Captains
Elwes
Timpson
Fenner
Brabazon
Handfield
Cowley
Indsey
Raymond
Seix

Captain Lieutenant
Rowland

Lieutenants
Handfield
Shawe
Porter
Dumarasque
Borland
Hugh Wallace
Reid

Abercrombie
Tone
Lindsay
Brick
Curries
White
Aked
Dowling
John Wallace
Craven
Dunn
McDonald
Smith

Chaplain
Jones

Adjutant
Dumarasque

Quartermaster
Abercrombie

Surgeon
Wightman

Mate
McAlpin

Agents
Cox, Mair, and Cox

Twenty-Third (Regiment) or Royal Welsh Fusiliers

Colonel Sir William Howe
Lieutenant Colonel Balfour
Major McKenzie

Captains
Temple
Gibbons
Smythe
Keppel
Champagne
Saumurez
Peter
Apthorp
Drewry

Captain Lieutenant
Blacke

1st Lieutenants
Brown
Baynton
Chapman
Moir
Banet
Calvert
Campbell
Wallis
Price
Tuckey
Hennis
Markland

2nd Lieutenants
Saltonstall
Guyon
Partridge
Montresor
Innes
Fraser
Robinson
Hodsworthy
Place

Chaplain
Berdmore

Adjutant
Watson

Surgeon
Robertson

Agents
Cox, Mair, and Cox

**Twenty-Fourth
Regiment of Foot**

Colonel Taylor
Lieutenant Colonel
Balcaras
Major Agnew
Captains
  Master
  Pilmar
  Verchild
  Jones
  Beacroft
  Jamaison
  Blake
  Ferguson
  Coote
Captain Lieutenant
  Campbell
Lieutenants
  Bibby
  Cotter
  St. Eloy
  Johnson
  Doyle
  Freeman

  Eirie
  Stiel
  Spencer
  Reed
  Ferguson
  Forester
Ensigns
  Power
  Stowe
  Pringle
  Lindsay
  Kyrwood
  Foster
  Merida
  De Chambault
Chaplain
  Church
Adjutant
  Caladine
Quartermaster
  Ferguson
Surgeon
  Sone
Agents
  Mr. Roberts and
Son

Thirty-Third
Regiment of Foot

Colonel Cornwallis
Lieutenant Colonel
Webster
Major Dansey
Captains
  Campbell
  Eustace
  Gore
  Oaks
  Manley
  Kerr
  Greening
  Cornwallis
  Cotton
Captain Lieutenant
  Ingram
Lieutenants
  Nutt
  Salwin
  Beaver
  Jones
  Innes
  McDonald
  Collington

Ward
Curson
Wyngard
Norfordf
Harvay
Leger
Ensigns
  Fenwik
  Kelly
  Manly
  Gore
  Hughes
  Lundreth
Chaplain
  Grisdale
Adjutant
  Fox
Quartermaster
  Warde
Surgeon
  Cleland
Agents
  Messrs. Meyricks

Thirty-Seventh Regiment of Foot

Colonel Sir Guy Coote
Lieutenant Colonel Abercromby
Major Couseau
Captains
Montgomery
Douglas
Beckwith
Coote
Hamilton
Savage
McKenzie
Cooke
Cameron
Captain Lieutenant
Dalton
Lieutenants
Cooke
Lightburn
Saunderson
Leigh
Brown
Thompson

Pope
Digby
Fletscher
O'Conner
Venters
Beckwith
Ensigns
Edwards
Fitzgerald
Braban
Passingham
Ross
Chaplain
Toosey
Adjutant
Thompson
Quartermaster
Venters
Surgeon
Johnson
Agents
John and George Hesse, Esqs.

Lists

Thirty-Eighth
Regiment of Foot

Colonel Sir Robert
Pigot
Lieutenant Colonel
Fox
Major Calheart
Captains
Macginis
Christie
Davies
Pottinger
Boyd
Handfield
Millet
Cleghorn
Captain Lieutenant
Sergeant
Lieutenants
Ourdon
Ashe
Mmacewen
Ruaton
Campbell
Johnston
Croker

Godere
Fowler
Silvaugh
Brownriff
Swiney
Ord
Cooke
Hales
Robinson
Forest
Kent
Winlerton
Wyvilla
Maxwell
Chaplain
Willis
Adjutant
Silvaugh
Quartermaster
Fowler
Surgeon
Mitchel

**Forty-Second
Regiment of Foot**

Colonel Murray
Lieutenant Colonel
Stirling
Major Graham
Captains
Smith
Grant
Dalrymple
Macdowal
McPerson
Peebles
Anstruter
Captain Lieutenant
Rutherford
Lieutenants
Potts
Franklin
Drummond
McGregor
Innes
Cumine
Campbell
Graham
William Fraser

Ritchie
Douglas Campbell
Alston
Dickson
Crammond
Grant
Stewart
McLean
Stirling
McDonald
Fraser
Alexander Grant
Young
Calender
Sutherland
William Fraser, Sr.
William Fraser, Jr.
Chaplain
McLaggan
Adjutant
Fraser
Quartermaster
McLean
Surgeon
Robertson
Mates
Stewart
Smith

Agent - Mr. Anderson
Forty-Third
Regiment of Foot

Colonel Carey
Lieutenant Colonel
Marsh
Major Ferguson
Captains
  Thomson
  Cameron
  Innes
  Thorn
  Blakeley
  Hatfield
  McLean
  Miller
  Todd
Captain Lieutenant
  Morris
Lieutenants
  Losack
  Daunbar
  May
  Roberts
  Vignoles
  Skeene
  Kerr

  Drammond
  Hill
  Sherlok
  Crichton
Ensigns
  Price
  Dickens
  East
  Clark
  Dennis
  Fenton
  Millington
Chaplain
  Taylor
Adjutant
  Hill
Quartermaster
  Kennedy
Surgeon
  McIntire
Mate
  Waugh
Agents
  Messrs. Cox, Mair, and Cox

**Forty-Seventh
Regiment of Foot**

Colonel G. Carleton
Lieutenant Colonel
Sutherland
Major Irving
Captains
Sheriffe
Alcock
Douglas
Gamble
Featherstone
England
Aubrey
Mountain
Marr
Captain Lieutenant
Storey
Lieutenants
Irvine
England
Baldwin
Warde
Rotten
Eyre
Caulfield

Dupont
Fox
French
Eccleston
Banbury
Ford
Ensigns
Blond
Hamilton
Moore
Squitre
Stephens
Hill
Mountaine
Carruthers
Chaplain
Witty
Adjutant
Poe
Quartermaster
Paaton
Surgeon
Dubbin
Agents
Adair and Bullock

Fifty-Fourth
Regiment of Foot

Colonel Frederick
Lieutenant Colonel
Bruce
Major Eyre
Captains
Breese
Bachop
Moore
Lane
Bronfield
French
Addenbroke
Powell
Captain Lieutenant
Darby
Lieutenants
Nichols
Lagard
Goldsmith
Montgomery
Daunt
Palmer
Brisbane
Graeme
Colvill

Griffin
Brackenburg
Seton
Blount
Ensigns
Campbell
Wilkinson
Hall
Frederick
Overing
Lupton
Chaplain
Davis
Adjutant
Hall
Quartermaster
Campbell
Surgeon
Gordon
Mate
Campbell
Agents
Messrs. Ross and
Gray

Fifty-Seventh Regiment of Foot

Colonel Irwine
Lieutenant Colonel Campbell
Major Brownlow
Captains
  Long
  Willington
  Dalrymple
  Thompson
  Balfour
  Waldron
  Graham
  Nugent
  Waugh
Captain Lieutenant
  Dawson
Lieutenants
  Schaak
  Murray
  Roberts
  Grant
  Taylor
  Clair
  Thomson
  Jackson

Dorrington
Hogg
Ovens
Fitzgerald
Ensigns
  Kerr
  Blood
  Arnott
  Vaamorel
  Waldron
  Watson
Chaplain
  Lumley
Adjutant
  Nunn
Quartermaster
  Mayal
Surgeon
  Davy
Mate
  Tarnball
Agents
  Messrs. Cox, Mair, and Cox

**Sixtieth Regiment
Of Foot, or Royal
Americans
(3rd Battalion)**

Colonel Amherst
Lieutenant Colonel
Dalling
Major Lloyd
Captains
  Provost
  Barrois
  Rivers
  Duffield
  Carden
  Breure
  De Diemar
  Sneyder
  Hughes
Captain Lieutenant
  Brely
Lieutenants
  Lookell
  Gordon
  Ward
  Devisme
  Crousax
  Haldimand

  Meggs
  Floyer
  Hesselberg
  Plumer
Ensigns
  Dalling
  Walsh
  Rogers
  Eberhard
  John August
Prevost
  Prevost
  Broadstreet
  Gould
  McKenzie
  Hulet
Chaplain
  Schlaeter
Adjutant
  Gordon
Quartermaster
  Genevay
Surgeon
  Sommers
Agents
  Messrts. Ross and Gray

Lists

Sixtieth Regiment Of Foot, or Royal Americans 4th Battalion)

Colonel Amherst
Lieutenant Colonel
Prevost
Major Glazier
Captains
Faesch
Murray
Shaw
Stevenson
Robertson
Christie
Hutchins
Barrard
Erskine
Captain Lieutenant
Montrond
Lieutenants
Luchenwiz
Loup
Britenback
Graham
McDonald
Mackenzie

Porbrik
Kerarsley
Wright
Barde
Bonnipace
Moncrieffe
Ensigns
Clair
Facio
Cartwright
Elphinston
Mueller
Field
Prevost
Clarke
Martin
Chaplain
Bowe
Quartermaster
Wright
Surgeon
Henderson
Agents
Messrs. Ross and
Gray

32

Lists

Sixty-Second Regiment of Foot

Colonel Mathew
Lieutenant Colonel Anstruther
Major Harnage

Captains
Marley
Shrimpton
Bunbury
Bailey
Harrington
Hawker
Nash
Sotheron
Hall

Captain Lieutenant
Vallancy

Lieutenants
Jones
Wilkinson
Blackall
Coane
Bromhaed
Wybrants
Blacker
Lord Torpichen
Naylor
James
Harvay
Newton

Ensigns
Danterroche
Blood
Wier
Fisher
Pack
Parker
Anstruther
Oldham

Chaplain
George

Adjutant
Vallancy

Quartermaster
Bromhaed

Surgeon
Moodie

Agents
Messrs. Cox, Mair, and Cox

Lists

Sixty-Third Regiment Of Foot

Colonel Grant
Lieutenant Colonel
Paterson
Major Wemyss
Captains
  Lysaght
  McKinnon
  Mallon
  Jones
  Stewart
  Leger
  Ball
  Rawdon
Captain Lieutenant
  Roberts
Lieutenants
  Marshall
  Lyster
  Money
  Birmingham
  Starke
  Baillis
  Campbell
  Peers
  Robertson

  Macleroth
Ensigns
  Lloyd
  Impet
  Bresset
  Mullins
  Beacroft
  Green
  Nash
  Wright
Chaplain
  Powell
Adjutant
  Starke
Quartermaster
  Dallton
Surgeon
  Jefferson
Agents
  Messrs. Cox, Mair, and Cox

**Sixty-Fourth
Regiment of Foot**

Colonel Pomeroy
Lieutenant Colonel
Leslie
Major McLeroth
Captains
Bowes
Lewis
Snowe
Strong
Gregory Kelly
Laton
Simondson
Kelly
Jacob
Captain Lieutenant
Russel
Lieutenants
Gratton
Gilsillan
Torriano
Wyngard
Rochford
Boswell
Hutchinson
Graham

Hoysted
Wright
Steadman
Mercer
Cowell
Ensigns
Makerell
Wood
Barr
Warner
D'Arcy
Caplain
Bell
Adjutant
Mercer
Quartermaster
Graton
Surgeon
Howard
Agents
Messrs. Meyricks

Seventieth Regiment
Of Foot

Colonel Tryon
Lieutenant Colonel
Bruce
Major Hicks
Captains
  Skinner
  Hewett
  Ewall
  Lee
  Banks
  Johnstone
  Irving
  Sharpe
  Meredith
Captain Lieutenant
  Nicoll
Lieutenants
  Hall
  Williamson
  Johnstone
  Brakenbury
  Phillips
  Hicks
  Morden
  Swymmer

  Tovey
  Bartlett
  Nares
Ensigns
  Bethune
  Holland
  Obins
  Phillips
  Morris
Chaplain
  Parslow
Adjutant
  Tovey
Quartermaster
  Hutchinson
Surgeon
  Lighthuzer
Agents
  Mr. Elwin, Grays
Inn

Seventy-First Regiment of (Highland) Foot

Colonel Fraser
Lieutenant Colonel Campbell
Lieutenant Colonel McDonald
Major McArthur
Major Fraser

Captains
Campbell
Laurie
Robert Campbell
Innes
Colin Campbell
Duncanson
Skelly
McIntosh
Baird
Hutchinson
McDonald
Sutherland
Monro
Robertson
Hugh Campbell
Fraser

Menzies
McLeod

Captain Lieutenant
Nairne

Lieutenants
Nairne
Fraser
Balnoves
Robert McDonald
Ross
McLean
Hamilton
Walkinshaw
McBean
Gordon
Robert Campbell
Cameron
Baine
Grant
James Campbell
Lieth
William Gordon
Willson
Hewitson
Marchieson
Watts
McKenzie
Alexander Fraser

Lists

John McKenzie
McLeod
Forbes
Grant
Thomas Fraser
Storey
Abercrombie
Grant
Smollet Campbell
Colin Campbell
Angus McDonald
McCaskil
Robertson
Archibald Campbell
Angus McDonald
Willington
Flint
McPherson
Edward Fraser

Ensigns
Stuart
Duncan Campbell
Robert Campbell
Dewarr
Sutherland
McKenzie
McLeod
Malcolm Grant

Cameron
McDougal
McIntosh
McBean
McTavish
Angus Cameron
Forbes
William McLeod
John Grant

Chaplain
Blair

Adjutant
Archibald Campbell

Quartermaster
Colin Campbell

Surgeons
Colin Chisholme
John Stuart

Mates
Ochiltree
Gray
Barns
Jackson

Seventy-Sixth Regiment of (Highland) Foot

Lieutenant Colonel McDonnel
Major Donaldson
Major John, Earl of Caithness

Captains
Bruce
McDonald
A. Mont. Cunninghame
Barclay
Fraser
William Cunninghame
Cameron

Lieutenants
Alexander McDonald
Allan McDonald
Martin
McDonnel
Agnas McDonald
Donald McDonald
McQueen

McLuchlan
McLean
MacKay
James McDonald
McKenzie
Shaw
Marrae
Stuart
Lamont
Robertson
Trail
Rose
Simon McDonald
Wemyss

Ensigns
Colin McDonald
Bruce
Colin McDonald
McColme
Duncan McDonald
Grant

Chaplain - McDonald
Adjutant - McKay
Quartermaster
Stuart
Surgeon - McLure
Agents - Messrs. Bishop and Brummel

Eightieth Regiment of Foot, or Edinburgh Volunteers

Colonel Erskine
Lieutenant Colonel
Dundas
Major Maxwell
Captains
Napier
Murray
Kinloch
Tyller
Hawthorn
Cammine
Arbuthnot
Lieutenants
McDonald
Nicolson
Heston
Armstrong
Jamieson
Dickson
Robb
Learmouth
Stilke
Balvaird
Thomson

Gibson
Heron
Forrester
Logan
Veitch
Cunninghame
Hunter
Clark
Stewart
Hope
Stoddart
Anderson
George Cunninghame
Chaplain
Dick
Adjutant
Nicolson
Quartermaster
Wells
Surgeon
Frier

Lists

Eighty-Second Regiment of Foot

Colonel McDean
Lieutenant   Colonel
Canning
Major Craig
Major Robertson
Captains
McPherson
Nisbitt
Pitcairn
Mair
Baird
Royal
Dunllap
Captain Lieutenant
Moore
Lieutenants
Carfrae
Reeves
Rutherford
Maxwell
Graham
Imrie
Fairie
Anderson
McDonald

Leslie
McPherson
Wellwood
McNiel
Dunlop
Cunninghame
Hamilton
Fraser
Evan McPherson
Kennevie
Ensigns
Duncanson
Dumas
Robertson
Stewart
Stewart
McPherson
Evan McPherson
McDonald
Chaplain
Cochrane
Adjutant
Wellwood
Quartermaster
Carfrae
Surgeon
Innes
Mate - Clarke

41

Eighty-Fourth Regiment of Foot, or Royal Night (2nd Battalion)

Colonel Clinton
Major Small
Captains
Helander McDonald
McKinnon
Alan McDonald
Allan McDonald
Ducan McDonald
McLean
John McDonald
Niel Campbell
Captain Lieutenant
Lundie
Lieutenants
Bliss
Lachlan McLean
McDonnel
Ken McDonald
Murray
Robertson
James McDonald
Fraser

Hector McLean
John McDonald
Hawkins
Ensigns
Alexander McLean
Donald McDonald
Robertson
Ducan Campbell
McQuary
Angus McDonald
Archibald Campbell
Chaplain
McKenzie
Adjutant
Hector McLean
Quartermaster
Ay. McDonald
Surgeon
Boyd
Mate
Cameron
Agents
Cox, Mair, and Cox

Lists

General Staff of the
Hessian Troops in
North America

Lieutenant General
and Commander Baron
Von Knyphausen

Adjutant Generals
Major Bauermeister
Captains
Doernberg
Beckwith
Lieutenants
Marquard
von Bassewiz
Von Crammond
Major General
von Lossberg
Adjutant - Lieutenant
Melzheimer
Major General
von Bose
Adjutant - Lieutenant
Henel
Major General
von Kospoth
Adjutant - Lieutenant

Marquard
Major General
von Hagenberg
Adjutant - Lieutenant
Grae
Major General
von Gosen
Adjutant - Lieutenant
Westphal
Major General
von Knoblauch
Adjutant - Lieutenant
von Knoblauch
Brigadier General
von Bischhausen
General Quartermaster
Colonel von Coch-
enhausen
Deputy Quartermaster
Generals
Lieutenant von Gir-
encourt
Lieutenant von
Vomecourt

43

Lists

Brigade Majors
    Captain Werner
    Lieutenant Fuehrer
War Commissary and
General Auditor
    Motz
Royal Provost
    Lieutenant Riedel
Wagon Master General
    Schade
Reformed Chaplain
    Becker
Evangelical Chaplain
    Heller
Commissaries
    Johann G. Lorenz
    Richard Lorenz
War and General
Commissary
    Dane Jagdmeister
Commissary of Stores
    Ebert
General Hospital
Physicians
    Doctor Lauchard
    Doctor Michaelis
Hospital Chaplain
    Schreiber

Grand Surgeons
    Amelung
    Bauer
Purveyor
    Gelan
Clerks
    Schmid
    Mussel
    Schaefer
Surgeons
    Girard
    Wagner
    Claus
    Moeller
    Bauer
    Fleck
Apothecary
    Schirmer
Cooks
    Welgenhaussen
    Sander

Von Linsingen Grenadier Battalion

Lieutenant Colonel
von Linsingen
Captains
  von Webern
  von Plessen
  von Dinklage
  von Mallet
1st Lieutenants
  von Schuler
  Schraidt
  von Hegemann
2nd Lieutenants
  von Hartleben
  von Verschuer
  von Ende
  Dunker
  von Hanstein
  von Wangenheim
  Kersting
Adjutant
  Kleinschmidt
Quartermaster
  Broetke

Von Lengercke Grenadier Battalion

Lieutenant Colonel
von Lengercke
Captains
  Vogt
  von Gall
  Reuting
  von O'Reilly
1st Lieutenants
  von Kospoth
  von Trott
  Reis
  von Kospoth
  Haasmann
  von Leliva
2nd Lieutenants
  von Kospoth
  von Lossberg
  von Geyso
  Hartmann
Adjutant
  Kuntzseh
Quartermaster
  Spangenberg

Lists

Von Loewenstein Grenadier Battalion	**Graf Grenadier Battalion**
Lieutenant Colonel von Loewenstein	Lieutenant Colonel Graf
Captains	Captains
Wach	Bode
Mondorf	Neaamann
Klingender	Mertz
von Beisenroth	Hohenstein
1st Lieutenants	Hessenmueller
Kimm	1st Lieutenant
von Winzingerode	Muehlhaussen
Toepfer	Waldeck
Zinck	von Dalwigk
2nd Lieutenants	Fritsch
Briede	2nd Lieutenants
von Rabenau	Schenck
von Komrad	Juny
Descourdres	von Lahrbusch
von Hoben	Ensigns
von Geyson	Wiederhold
Adjutant	Schimelpfennig
Hille	Adjutant
Quartermaster	Brauns
Unger	Quartermaster
	Bauer

Leib Regiment

Colonel von Wurmb
Major von Stamford
Captains
  Metz
  von Milckau
  von Kroening
  von Long
  von Urff
1st Lieutenant
  Bode
2nd Lieutenants
  Ernst
  Germar
  Ludemann
  Wiederhold
Ensigns
  von Helmbold
  von Dalwigk
  von Sacken
  von der Lith
Adjutannt
  von Groening
Regimental Quarter-
Master
  Lotheissen

Auditor
  Wille
Regimental Surgeon
  Waldeck

Landgraf Regiment

Colonel von Keudel
Lieutenant Colonel
von Hanstein
  Major Eschwege
Captains
  Murarins
  Wolpert
  Ernst
2nd Lieutenants
  Goeddens
  von Seelhorst
  von Zanthier
  von Ende
  Wagener
Ensigns
  von Kleist
  von Hanstein
  Schoenewolf
  von Pappenheim
  von Roosing
  vm Berglassen
  Von Nolden

Lists

Adjutant
  Klingsoehr
Regimental Quarter-
Master
  Bockewitz
Chaplain
  Stern
Auditor
  Meissenlein
Regimental Surgeon
  Ahlaut

**Hereditary Prince
Regiment**

  Lieutenant Colonel
Fuchs
  Major Walden-
berger
Captains
  von Gall
  Laun
  Gebhard
  von Schallern
  Kummel
1st Lieutenant
  Haller
2nd Lieutenants

von Westerhagen
von Keudel
Pfaff
von Andersohn
Ungewitter
Ensigns
  Motz
  Schoenewolf
Adjutant
  Plumque
Chaplain
  Hausknecht
Regimental Surgeon
  Avemann

**Prince Charles
Regiment**

Captains
  Fischer
  Gerrstmann
  Spangenberg
  Steuber
  Hartert
  Beckers

2n^{d} Lieutenants
 Schmid
 von Trott
 von Doernberg
 Knoll
Ensigns
 von Trott
 von Eptinger
 Schmidt
 Roosing
Adjutant
 Beckert
Regimental Quartermaster
 Mssr. Pfaff
Regimental Surgeon
 Bauer

Von Ditfurth Regiment

Colonel von Westerhagen
 Lieutenant Colonel von Schuler
 Major von Bork

Captains
 von Malzburg
 von Malzburg
 Eygerding
 Schaeffer
2nd Lieutenants
 Haller
 von Bardeleben
 Valtejns
 von Trumbach
 Duncker
Ensigns
 Firhaber
 Brasser
 Wejel
 Schachter
 von Butlar
 Loray
Quartermaster
 Wende
Regimental Surgeon
 Limberger

Lists

Von Donop Regiment

Lieutenant Colonel
Hinte
  Major Wurmb
Captains
  Gissot
  von Donop
  Murhard
  Venator
  Geisler
2nd Lieutenants
  von Nagel, Sr.
  von Nagel, Jr.
  von Bardeleben
  von Freienhagen
  von Donop
  von Trott
Ensigns
  von Knoblauch
  von Lehrbach
  Murhard
Adjutant
  von Lepell
Regimental Quarter-master
  Zinn

Chaplain
  Coester
Auditor
  Heymel
Regimental Surgeon
  Stiegiliz

Von Lossberg Regiment

  Colonel von Loos
  Lieutenant Colonel
Schaeffer
  Major von Hanstein
Captains
  von Altenbockum
  von Wurmb
  Steding
  Kraft
2nd Lieutenants
  Scchwale
  Zoll
  Biel
  Moeller
Ensigns
  Grebe
  von Zengen

50

Ruthmann
Waldeck
von Luders
Hendorf
Kres
Kroen
Recorden
Regimental Quarter-
Master
   Haenser
Regimental Surgeon
   Oliva

**Von Knyphausen
Regiment**

   Colonel von Bork
   Lieutenant Colonel
Heimel
   Major von Stein
Captains
   von Loewenstein
   Baum
   Schimmelpfennig
   von Rueffurth
   von Wolop
   Vaupel
   Wiederhold

2nd Lieutenants
   Briede
   von Rieger
   von Luetzow
Ensigns
   von Drach
   Ritteer
   von Mueller
   Zimmermann
   Unger
Adjutant
   Sobbe
Regimental Quarter-
master
   Mueller
Chaplain
   Bauer
Auditor
   Mueller
Regimental Surgeon
   Pausch

Lists

Von Mirbach Regiment

Colonel von Rom-roth
Lieutenant Colonel Von Biesenroth
Major von Wilmow-sky

Captains
  Reichhhold
  Rodemann
  Rothe
  von Toll

1st Lieutenant
  Broeske

2nd Lieutenants
  von Boyneburg
  von Biesenroth
  von Drach
  Wisker
  Wiessenmueller
  von Biesingsleben
  Berner

Ensigns
  von Ehrenstein
  Fey
  Lange

Adjutant
  Rueffer

Regimental Quarter master
  Schmid

Chaplain
  Rernau

Auditor
  Heinemann

Regimental Surgeon
  Gechter

Von Bose Regiment

Colonel Von Muenchhausen
Major Dupuy

Captains
  Scheer
  von Stein
  Roll
  von Wilmowsky
  Eigenbrod

1st Lieutenants
  Schwaner
  Hoepfner
  Butte
  Geyso

2nd Lieutenants
   von Nezer
   von Burghof
Ensigns
   von Trott
   Brauns
   Runk
   Spangenberg
Adjutant
   Rode
Regimental Quarter-
master
   Strube
Regimental Surgeon
   Wuerfelmann

1st Lieutenant
   von May
2nd Lieutenants
   Studenroth
   Kienen, Sr.
   Kienen, Jr.
   Fleck
   Wernik
   Broeske
Ensigns
   Werner
   Mathaeus
Gombrecht
   Boecking
   Goebel

Marquis d'Angelelli Grenadier Battalion

   Colonel Koehler
   Major Endemann
Captains
   Bauer
   Salzmann
   Widdekind
   Feetz
   Stebel
   von Griesheim

Von Knoblauch Regiment

   Lieutenant Colonel
von Porbeck
   Major Goerbel
   Major von Ende
Captains
   Gundermann
   Heyemann
   Boedicker
   von Dalwigk

1st Lieutenant
  Koerber
2nd Lieutenants
  Goebel
  Abel
  Koerber
  Gesner
Ensigns
  Justi
  Weissdenborn
  Stuekradt
  Dick
  Peternell
Chaplain
  Grimmel
Auditor
  Schanz
Regimental Surgeon
  Krupp

**Von Huyne
Regiment**

Colonel Kurze
Lieutenant Colonel
Hillebrand
Major Martini

Captains
  Sonneborn
  Reinhart
  Hoecker
  Heilemann
  Stueck
1st Lieutenants
  Roepenack
  Kuhl
2nd Lieutenants
  Krupp
  Scheuch
  Hillebrand
Ensigns
  Eckhard
  Hartung
  Martini
  Reinhart
Adjutant
  Ataerklof
Regimental Quarter-
master -   Kleinschmid
Chaplain - Kuemmel
Auditor - Kleinsteuber
Regimental Surgeon
  Witte

Lists

Von Seitz Regiment

Colonel von Seitz
Lieutenant Colonel
Kitzel
Major Schallern
Captains
Langenschwarz
Bode
Justi
Henklemann
Sandrock
Muench
Oehlhans
2nd Lieutenants

2nd Lieutenants
Knies
Vieth
von Boyneburg
Paul
Ensigns
Koerber
Maus
Petri
Stolzenbach
Langenschwarz
Adjutant
Fenner
Regimental Quarter-

master
Spangenberg
Regimental Surgeon
Heimreich

Von Buenau Regiment

Colonel von Bue-
nau
Lieutenant Colonel
Schaeffer
Major Platte
Major Boecking
Captains
Goebel
Noltenius
Firnhaber
1st Lieutenants
Becker
Feldner
Werner
2nd Lieutenants
Frohn
Bauer
Schaeffer
Grebe
Adjutant
Gombert

Regimental Quarter-
master
   Strate
Regimental Surgeon
   Beck

Jaeger Corps

   Lieutenant Colonel
von Wurmb
   Lieutenant Colonel
von Prueschenk
   Major von Wurmb
Captains
   Ewald
   Hanger
   Heinrichs
   von Bodungen
   von Rau
   von Donop
   von Wangenheim
1st Lieutenants
   von Hagen, Sr.
   von Hagen, Jr.
   Wolf
   von Winzingerode
   von Messy

2nd Lieutenants
   Schaeffer
   Bueckel
   Cornelius
   Bohle
   Flies
Adjutant
   Kellerhaus
Regimental Quarter-
master
   Beckmann
Auditor
   Wisker
Regimental Surgeon
   Henke

Lists

<u>Artillery Corps</u>

Lieutenant Colonel
Eitel
<u>Captains</u>
Schleestein
Krug
1st <u>Lieutenant</u>
Kaiser
2nd <u>Lieutenants</u>
Fischer
Goercke
Schaeffer
Schwarzenberg
Schirmer
Schmid
Engelhgard
Korngiebel
<u>Commissary</u>
Wiederhold

Lists

List of Ansbach-Bayreuth Officers and Staff

1st, or Ansbach, or von Voit Regiment

Colonel
  Von Voit
Major
  von Seitz
Captains
  von Ellrodt
  von Stain (or Stein)
  von Metsch
1st Lieutenants
  von Keller
  Marschall von Biberstein
  Trechsel von Teafstetten
  von Diemar
  Prechtel
  Guttenberg
2nd Lieutenants
  Drexel
  Minameier

Baumann
Duehlemann
von Fabrice
Halbmeier
Beier
Lower Staff
  Lieutenant and Auditor - Rummel
  Regimental QM - Meier
  Regimental Surgeon - Rapp
  Chaplain - Wagner
  Artillery Captain - Hofmann

Lists

Field Jaeger Regiment

Colonel
Baron von Reitzenstein

Captains
von Waldenfels
von Roeder
Tritschler von Falkenstein
von Koenitz
Von Wurmb

Captain Lieutenants
Baron von Reitzenstein
von Schoenfeld

1st Lieutenants
von der Heydte
Baron von Reitzenstein
von Diemar

2nd Lieutenants
Bartholomei
Kling
Deahna
Bush
Bach
von Hiller

von Eyb
von Massenbach
Count von Bubna and Lititz

Adjutants
Otto
Frank
Neithardt von Gneisenau
Morg

Lower Staff
Lieutenant and Auditor - Frisch
Regimental QM - Haussellt
Regimental Surgeon - Arnold
Chaplain - Erb

59

2nd, or Bayreuth, or von Seybothen Regiment
Colonel
    Von Seybothen
Major
    Von Beust
Captains
    von Eyb
    von Molitor
    von Quesnoy
Captain Lieutenant
    Seidel
1st Lieutenants
    von Adelsheim
    von Streit
    von Weitershausen
    von Tunderfeld
    von Altenstein
    von Weinhart
2nd Lieutenants
    von Cyriazy
    Lindemeier
    Hirsch
    Graebner
    Matolay
    Popp

Lower Staff

Lieutenant and Auditor - Pflug
Regimental QM - Daig
Regimental Surgeon - Schneller
Chaplain - Erb

List of the Officers of the Provincial Troops Raised in the Southern Districts of North America

General and Staff Officers

Brigadier Generals
DeLancey
Arnold
Skinner
Inspector General
Innis, Esq.
Deputy Inspectoir Generals
Captain Rooke
Captain Bridgham
Lieutenant Hugh
Lieutenant Gordon
Muster Master General
Winslow, Esq.
Deputy Muster Master Generals
In New York -
Chipman

In South Carolina -
Brice, Esq.
Major of Brigade
Wallop
Paymaster of the Provincial Troops
Smith, Esq.

Quen's American Rangers

Lieutenant Colonel
Simcoe
Major Armstrong
Captains
McKay
Dunlop
Murray
Agnew
Smith
Shaw
Stevenson
McCrea
Keer
McGill
Whitlok

Lists

Lieutenants
- Ormond
- Fitzpatrick
- Mathewson
- Dunlop
- Alllen
- Howe
- McKan
- Atkinson
- Murray
- Pindred
- McKay
- Holland
- John Dunlop

Ensigns
- Armstrong
- Miller
- Eoss
- Calender
- Murray
- Wardlaw
- Munday
- Jarvis
- Armstrong

Chaplain
- Agnew

Quartermaster
- Mathewson

Adjutant
- Ormond

Surgeon
- Kellock

Cavalry

Captains
- Saunders
- Wickham
- Shanck
- Cook

Lieutenants
- McNabb
- Spencer
- Wilson
- Lawler, Adjutant

Cornets
- Merret
- Woolsey
- Jones
- Clayton

Lists

Volunteers of Ireland

Colonel Lord Rawdon
Lieutenant Colonel Doyle
Major Campbell
<u>Captains</u>
Doyle
Hastings
Barry
King
Blacker
McMahone
<u>Captain Lieutenant</u>
Dalton
<u>Lieutenants</u>
Valancy
Procker
Bradstreet
Munro
Jewell
Bingham
Moffatt
Gellespie
Black

<u>Ensigns</u>
Gilbourne
Cunningham
Whitely
Ransford
Flynn
Thompson
Sergeant
Cordner
<u>Chaplain</u>
Barker
<u>Adjutant</u>
Keens
<u>Quartermaster</u>
Stater
<u>Surgeon</u>
Armstrong
<u>Mate</u>
Hill

Lists

New York Volunteers

Lieutenant Colonel
Commandant Shereden

Captains
  Kane
  Coffin
  Johnston
  Gray
  Bars
  Cameron
  Althause

Lieutenants
  McGregor
  Munro
  Debeck
  McLean
  Peterson
  Hunt

Ensigns
  Walker
  Cumming
  Althause
  Townsend
  Cameron

Chaplain - Brown
Adjutant - Townsend
Surgeon - Gibbs

Royal Fencible Americans

Lieutenant Colonel
Commandant Gorham
Major Batt

Captains
  Burns
  Studholm

Captain Lieutenant
  Bailey

1st Lieutenants
  Wilson
  Sharman
  Acheson
  Walker
  Conner

2nd Lieutenants
  Tongue
  Street
  Sutherland
  Gorham

Chaplain - Ecceleston
Adjutant - Clinch
Quartermaster - Spears
Surgeon - Callen

Nova Scotia Volunteers	**Brigadier General DeLancey's Brigade**
Colonel Legge	**First Battallion**
Captains	
Monck	Brigadier General
Green	DeLancey
Solomon	Lieutenant Colonel
Cunningham	Cruger
Vappel	Major Gree
Lieutenants	Captains
Tawson	Galbreath
Pringle	Smith
Morris	Roorbank
Ensigns	James French
Cusses	French
Needham	McDonald
Cunningham	Captain Lieutenant
Fitzwilliams	Kerr
	Lieutenants
* * * * * * *	Rooney
	Hays
	McPherson
	Cunningham
	Ensigns
	Old
	Wormley
	Suple

Boyle
Chaplain
Bowden
Quartermaster
Rogers
Surgeon
Smith
Mate
Cornwall

Second Battalion

Lieutenant Colonel
DeLancey
Major Bowden
Captains
Dunbar
Hallet
Hatch
Moore
Campbell
Captain Lieutenant
Potts
Lieutenants
McMillen
Hallet
Campbell
Cameron

Lister
Griffiths
Broocke
Ensigns
Ferguson
Brewerton
McDermot
Chaplain
Field
Adjutant
Cameron
Quartermaster
Potts
Surgeon
Johnson

Third Battalion

Colonel Ludlow
Lieutenant Colonel
Hewlett
Major D'Ueber
Captains
Allison
Hewlett
Lester
Willett
Miles

Lieutenants
  Clowes
  Smith
  John Clowes
  Evans
  Samuel Clowes
Ensigns
  McFarland
  Brown
  Barnum
  Montgomery
Chaplain
  Walter
Adjutant
  Clark
Quartermaster
  Floyd
Surgeon
  Doughty
Mate
  Wilson

**King's American
Regiment**

  Colonel Fanning
  Lieutenant Colonel
Campbell

Major Grant
Captains
  DePeyster
  Atwood
  Gray
  Clements
  Cornwall
  Livingston
  Chapman
Captain Lieutenant
  DePeyster
Lieutenants
  Wightmann
  McLeod
  Campbell
  Hustice
  Sargent
  Read
  Barn
  Smith
  MacKay
  Cox
  Fanning
Ensigns
  Young
  Grant
  Budd
  Harden Brook

Purdy
Barker
Mecan
Chaplain
  Seabury
Adjutant
  Cruckeninks
Quartermaster
  Thomas
Surgeon
  Tucker
Mate
  Drummond

**Prince of Wales'
American Regiment**

Colonel Brown
Lieutenant Colonel
Pattison
  Major Carden
Captains
  Bowen
  Lymann
  Maxwell
  Holland
  Hoyt
  Collett

Bridgwater
Captain Lieutenant
  McNeil
Lieutenants
  Shanks
  Hoyt
  Waecler
  McDonald
  Conroy
  Ambrose
  Lindsey
  O'Neal
Ensigns
  Keatring
  Ness
  Wellrop
  Holland
  Garret
  Place
  Bridgham
Chaplain
  Pinton
Adjutant
  Ness
Quartermaster
  Hoyt
Surgeon
  Thomas

Lists

**Brigadier General
Cortland Skinner's
Brigade of
New Jersey Volunteers**

First Battalion

Colonel Skinner
Lieutenant Colonel
Barton
Major Mellidge
Captains
  Crowell
  Cougle
  Taylor
  Shaw
  Nealon
Lieutenants
  Hutchingson
  Cunliff
  Haggerty
  Lawrence
  Leonard
  Hedden
  Thompson
Ensigns
  Read
  Brittain

Ansley
Milledge
Moody
Jewett
Barton
Adjutant
  Hedden
Surgeon
  Johnson

Second Battalion

Lieutenant Colonel
Morris
  Major Colden
Captains
  McLeas
  McLeod
  Campbell
  Bleau
  Stainforth
Captain Lieutenant
  Menzies
Lieutenants
  Dumont
  Parker
  Morrison
  Wilson

69

Stephenson
Prritchard
Lambert
French
Ensigns
   Bleau
   Legrange
Chaplain
   Rowland
Adjutant
   Legrange
Quartermaster
   Morrison
Surgeon
   Earle

Third Battalion

Lieutenant Colonel
Allen
   Major Drummond
Captains
   Lee
   Harrison
   Cocens
   Barberie
   Campbell
   Thatcher

Hunicke
Captain Lieutenant
   Steele
Lieutenants
   Jenkins
   Chew
   Harrison
   Lycon
   Troup
   Hatton
   Combs
Ensigns
   Camp
   Willis
   Combs
   Swanton
   Thomson
   Shannon
Adjutant
   Jenkins
Quartermaster
   Folker
Surgeon
   Peterson
Mate
   Campbell

Fourth Battalion

Lieutenant Colonel
Commandant Buskirk
  Major Van Cartland
Captains
  van Allen
  Ryerson
  Rutan
  Buskirk
Lieutenants
  Earle
  Serciniere
  Simondson
  van Buskirk
  Hyslop
  van Orden
Ensigns
  Earle
  van Cartland
  Storrel
  Cole
  Cooper
  Jewett
Chaplain
  Batwell
Quartermaster
  Sorrel

Surgeon
  Hammel

King's Orange Rangers

Lieutenant Colonel
Bayard
  Major Dewint
Captains
  Brace
  McDonald
  Howard
  DeMeyno
  Bayard
  Rotton
  van Buskirk
Lieutenant
  McLeod
  Rorison
  McDonald
  Bethell
  James
  Cummings
  Stewart
  Uniacke
  Dawson

Lists

Ensigns
  Grandidier
  Campbell
  Jackson
  Cameron
  McKenzie
  van Buskirk
Chaplain
  Townsend
Adjutant
  Jackson
Quartermaster
  Bethell
Surgeon
  Fraser

Loyal American Regiment

Colonel Robinson
Lieutenant Colonel
Robinson
  Major Barclay
Captains
  Hatch
  Robinson
  Kollock
  Caleb Fowler

Wilmot
Fowler
Howeson
Capain Lieutenant
  Bailey
Lieutenants
  Fletcher
  Ward
  Barbarie
  Haggeford
  Robinson
  Allair
  Henderson
  Colburn
  Ward
Ensigns
  Swords
  Fowler
  Apthorp
  Caleb Fowler
  Robinson
  Cunningham
  Morrison
Chaplains
  Beardsley
  Cunningham
Quartermaster
  Colbourn

Lists

Surgeon
Hatchell

Independent Companies

Captains
  Curganven
  Hierlihy
  McMullen
  Osborn
Lieutenants
  Kennedy
  Wheaton
  Wetmore
  Hendersson
  Etter
Ensigns
  Noble
  Wheaton
  Stuart

Loyal New Englanders

Lieutenant Colonel and Captain Wightman

Lieutenant
  Holland
Ensign
  Whiteman

British Legion

Lieutenant Colonel Commandant Tarleton
Major Cochran
Captains
  Edwards
  Rousselet
  Stewart
  Miller
1st Lieutenants
  McCrumman
  McPherson
  Donnavan
  McLeod
  McDonald
2nd Lieutenants
  Miller
  Seaton
  Campbell
Chaplain
  McLeod
Adjutant

Lists

Taylor
Quartermaster
McDonald
Mate
Skinner

Cavalry

Captains
Kinlooh
James
Novendon
Lieutenants
Chapman
Vernon
Cornets
Swain
Robins
Adjutant
Lergin

Maryland Loyalists

Lieutenant Colonel
Commandant Calmers
Major McDonald
Captains

Dulany
Jones
Frisby
Kennedy
Kay
Coster
Lieutenants
Niller
Parker
Townsend
Inglis
Stirling
Ensigns
Stirling
Jones
Munro
Cannon
Henley
Coffman
Chaplain
Patterson
Adjutant
Miller

74

Lists

Pennsylvania Loyalists

Lieutenant Colonel
Commandant Allen
Major Vacat
Captains
  Kearney
  Colden
  Stephens
  Swift
Lieutenants
  Baynton
  Holt
  Currie
Ensigns
  Harden
  McMichael
  Todd
Chaplain
  Odell
Adjutant
  Currie
Quartermaster
  Holt
Surgeon
  Christal

South Carolina Loyalists

Colonel Innes
Lieutenant Colonel
Robertson
Major McLairn
Adjutant
  Lindsay
Quartermaster
  Cooper

Florida Rangers

Lieutenant Colonel
Commandant Brown
Captains
  Wylly
  Smith
  Marshal
  Roworth
  Lawe
Lieutenants
  Cameron
  Brown
  Provost
  Ellis
  Hybert

Lists

Ensigns
  Anderson
  Smith
  Jones
  Simcokes
Chaplain
  Stewart
Adjutant
  Brown
Quartermaster
  Cornish
Surgeon
  Allan

**Governor
Wentworth's
Volunteers**

Captain
  Murray
Lieutenant
  Williams
Adjutant
  Oliver
Quartermaster
  Fulton

**Bucks County
Light Dragoons**

Captains
  Sandford
  Watson
Lieutenant
  Willet
Cornet
  Geran

Garrison Battalion

  Lieutenant Colonel
Commandant Donkin
  Major Anstruther
Captains
  Graant
  Ferrel
  Kelly
  Dalbunty
Lieutenants
  Baddely
  McGinnis
  Blandell
  Dorcus
  Davies
  Stewart

Hunt
Rio
Chisholm
Sutherland
Arch Blandell
Ensigns
John
Shadwell
Dunn
Chaplain
Inglis
Adjutant
Baddely
Quartermaster
Sutherland
Surgeon
Bell

King's Rangers

Lieutenant Colonel
Commandant Rogers
Major Rogers
Captains
Longstreet
Hatfield
Maddox
Stinson

Heyden
Bissonet
Welch
Betts
Captain Lieutenant
Mowat
Lieutenants
Oakerson
Throckmorton
Waller
Whiteworth
Wetherell
Jasley
Smith
Fletcher
Lippenoot
Ensigns
Robins
Beers
Taylor
Anderson
Stockton
Hutton

Royal North Carolina Volunteers

Lieutenant Colonel
Commandant Hamilton
Major Welsh
Captains
  Manson
  Legett
  Hamilton
  Hamilton
  McNiel
  McKinnon
Lieutenants
  McAlpine
  McRae
  Smith
  Martin
  Campbell
  Alex Campbell
Ensigns
  Shaw
  Atkins
  McLeod
  McKethan
Chaplain
  Ronaldson

Adjutant
  McLeod
Quartermaster
  Campbell
Surgeon
  McLeod
Mate
  Charleton

Georgia Volunteers

Major Commandant
Wright
  Hussars
Captain
  von Diemar
Lieutenants
  von Molitore
  Albus
Cornet
  Thompson

Lists

Guides and Pioneers	Seconded Officers On Half Pay
Colonel Robinson	
Captains	Colonel Cole
Aldington	Lieutenant Colonels
McPherson	Emmerich
Frazer	Ritzma
Sobrisky	Lawrence
Blaskowiz	Majors
McAlpine	Brown
Blair	Stockton
1st Lieutenants	Lynch
Kier	Timpany
McDonald	Stark
Wiliams	Vandyke
Browne	Captains
Stark	Alstone
Hunt	Vought
2nd Lieutenants	Stewart
McDonald	Hanley
Closs	Yelverton
Husband	Bowen
Benedict	Wilson
Adjutant	Houseal
Stark	Lindsay
Quartermaster	McLeod
Kier	McArthur
	Mackay

79

Lists

Alex McLeod	McLeod, Jr.
Sapponfield	Henry
Raymond	Barclay
Wiergan	Hatheway
Hooton	Chace
Terry	Michael
Clarke	William Frazer
Price	Craige
Rutherford	Robinson
McDonald	Lewis
Leggert	Airdell
John McLeod	Tupper
James McDonald	McKinnon
Knowland	Sterwart
Lieutenants	McKinnon
Munro	Ensigns
Frazer	Finnemore
Eck	Chase
Corey	Munro
Hume	Stretch
Wheaton	Morrison
Knight	Phinney
Brittle	Adjutant Chalmers
Pistoras	Quartermasters
Vernon	Nowland
Jonnes	Simm
Murchison	Surgeons -Dougan
McLeod	Bainbridge

Admirals of the Royal Navy

Admital of the Fleet
Lord Hawke
Admirals of the White
Forbes
Duke of Bolton
Sir Pye
Sir Rodney
Frankland
Earl of Northesk
Geary, Esq.
Young, Esq.
Admirals of the Blue
Sir Brett
Lord Edgecumbe
Keppel
Sir Douglas
Graves, Esq.
H.R.H., Duke of
Cumberland
Man, Esq.
Buckle, Esq.
Vice-Admirals of the Red
Gayton, Esq.
Harland

Pigot, Esq.
Howe
Vaughan, Esq.
Montagu, Esq.
Howe
Schuldham
Duff, Esq.
Vice-Admiral of the White
Reynolds, Esq.
Byron
Barton, Esq.
Barrington
Roddam, Esq.
Campbell, Esq.
Palliser, Esq.
Mackenzie, Esq.
Parker
Arbutnot, Esq.
Darby, Esq.
Vice-Admirals of the Blue
Gambier, Esq.
Lloyd, Esq.
Drake, Esq.
Parker, Sr., Esq.
Milbanke, Esq.
Hughes, Esq.

Lists

Evans, Esq.

Rear-Admirals of the Blue

Vincent, Esq.
Vernon
Edwards, Esq.
Digby, Esq.
Storr, Esq.
Rowley, Esq.
Graves, Esq.
Sir Ross

Rear-Admirals of the White

Webber, Esq.
Marlow, Esq.
Innes, Esq.
Langdon, Esq.
Hood, Esq.

Rear-Admirals of the Blue

Sir Ogle
Moore, Esq.
Drake, Esq.
Sir Hood
Sir Hughes
Kempenfell, Esq.

Rear-Admirals Superanuated on Half Pay at 17 Shillings, 6 Pence per Day

Bladwell
Dyve
Elliot
Fowke
Hardy
Hale
Knight
Knowler
Maplesden
Coffingwood
Edwards
Falkingham
Galbraith

Lists

Harrison
Jesseryes
John Knight
Lynne
Martin
Murray
Roswell
Weatwell
Robinson
Taylor

* * * * * * *

Lists

Rank of the Army and Navy	**Settled by the King in Council**
Land	**Sea**
Field Marshall	Admiral and Chief Commander
Generals of Horse and Foot	Admirals with Flags at Maintop
Lieutenant Generals	Vice-Admirals
Major Generals	Rear-Admirals
Brigadier Generals	Commodores
Colonels	Captains of Three Years
Lieutenant Colonels	Younger Captains
Majors	Masters and Commanders
Captains	Lieutenants

Lists

Description of Warships

Complement of Men and Metal in the Royal Navy

Ships off Three Decks

Guns	Men	1st	2nd	3rd	Above
100	850	42	24	12	6
90	750	32	18	12	6
80	600	32	18	9	6

Ships of Two Decks

Guns	Men	1st	2nd	3rd	Above
80	650	32	18		9
70	520	32	18		9
68	520				
66	520				
64	480	24	12		6
60	420	24	12		6
60	400	24	9		6
50	350	24	12		6
50	300	18	9		6
44	250	18	9		6

Ships of One Deck

Guns	Men	1st	2nd	3rd	Above
36	240	12			6
32	200	12			6
28	200	9			4
20	150	9			4

Lists

English Warships

A List of the Royal Navy of Great Britain

First Rate

Ships	Guns	Ships	Guns
Britania	100	*Royal George*	100
Victory	100		

Second Rate

Ships	Guns	Ships	Guns
Barfleur	90	*Blenheim*	90
Duke	90	*Formidable*	90
London	90	*Namur*	90
Neptune	90	*Ocean*	90
Prince George	90	*Princess Royal*	90
Queen	90	*Sandwich*	90
Union	90		

Third Rate

Ships	Guns	Ships	Guns
Africa	64	*Ajax*	64
Anson	64	*Alfred*	74
Alexander	74	*St. Albans*	64
Albion	64	*Alcide*	74
America	64	*Asia*	64
Arrogant	74	*Princess Amelia*	80
Bedford	74	*Belleisle*	64
Belllona	74	*Berwik*	74
Bienfaisant	64	*Boyne*	64

Lists

Burford	64	Cambridge	80
Canada	74	Centour	74
Cornwall	74	Courageous	74
Culloden	74	Cumberland	74
Defence	64	Dragon	74
Dublin	74	Edgar	74
Egmont	74	Elizabeth	74
Essex	64	Europa	64
Exeter	64	Fame	74
Foudroyant	80	Grafton	74
Hector	74	Hercules	74
Hero	74	Invincible	74
Intrepid	64	Kent	74
Lonox	74	Lion	64
Magnificent	74	Marlboro	74
Mars	74	Modeste	64
Monarch	74	Montague	74
Monmouth	64	Nonsuch	64
Norfolk	74	Oxford	70
Polyphemas	64	Prudent	64
Ramillies	74	Raisonable	64
Resolution	74	Revengere	64
Russel	74	Robust	74
Ruby	64	Royal Oak	74
Sterling Castle	64	Shrewsbery	74
Suffolk	74	Sultan	74
Superb	74	Temetaira	70
Terrible	74	Thunderer	74

Lists

Torbay	74	Trident	64
Triumph	74	Valiant	74
Prince of Wales	74	Warrior	74
Warspite	74	Royal William	84
Worcestor	64	Yarmouth	64

Fourth Rate

Achillies	60	St. Anne	60
Bristol	50	Centorion	50
Chatham	50	Conquestadore	60
Dreadnought	60	Dunkirk	60
Firme	60	Hannibal	60
Jupiter	50	Jersey	60
Isis	50	Leopard	60
Lanceston	60	Medway	60
Panther	60	Pembroke	60
Portland	50	Preston	50
Renown	50	Rippon	60
Romney	50	Salisbury	50
Windsor	60	Warwik	60

Fifth Rate

Acteon	44	Aeolus	32
Alarm	32	Amazon	32
Ambuscade	32	Andromeda	28
Appollo	32	Aquilon	28
Aurora	28	Boreas	28
Blonde	32	Bologne	32

Lists

Boston	32	Brilliant	36
Bruno	32	Charon	44
Charleston	32	Carysfort	28
Cleopatra	32	Convert	32
Coventry	28	Crescent	32
Cyclops	28	Danae	32
Diamond	32	Diana	32
Endymion	44	Enterprize	40
Emerald	32	Garland	26
Grayhound	28	Guadalupe	32
Hinchinbrook	28	Iris	32
Janus	44	Jason	32
Levant	28	Lizard	28
Lowestoffe	42	Licorn	32
LaPrudent	36	Laurel	28
Maidstone	28	Medea	28
Mercury	28	Milford	28
Niger	32	Oiscan	32
Pallas	36	Pearl	32
Pegasus	28	Pamona	28
Proserpine	28	Raleigh	32
Rainbow	44	Resource	28
Richmond	32	Roebuck	44
Romelus	44	Saphine	32
Sartine	32	Southampton	32
Solebay	28	Surprize	28
Stagg	32	Tartar	28
Triton	28	Thames	32

Lists

Thetis	32	*Tortoise*	32
Ulysses	44	*Venus*	36
Vestall	32	*Virginia*	32
Winchelsea	32		

Sixth Rate

Airadne	20	*Amphitrite*	32
Camel	20	*Champion*	24
Camilla	20	*Deal Castle*	24
Delaware	28	*Daphne*	20
Dromedary	26	*Fowey*	24
Galatea	20	*Hind*	20
Hyena	24	*Hydra*	24
Pandora	24	*Pelican*	24
Perseus	20	*Porcubine*	20
Porteus	26	*Scarborough*	20
Seaford	20	*Seahorse*	20
Squirrel	20	*Sphynx*	20
Sybil	20	*Suren*	24
Terpsichore	20	*Tortoise*	20
Unicorn	20	*Vigilant*	24
Wager	24		

Sloops

Albany	14	*Alderney*	10
Atalanta	16	*Alert*	10
Allegiance	18	*Avenger*	16
Badger	16	*Barbados*	14

Lists

Beaver	14	Bonetta	14
Camelion	16	Caecass	18
Cygnet	18	Dispatch	14
Delight	16	Endeavor	10
Fairy	14	Falcon	18
Favorite	16	Fly	14
Fortune	14	Fury	18
Hawke	10	Hazard	8
Helena	14	Hornet	16
Hound	14	Hunter	10
Kite	12	Lively	12
Loyalist	16	Lynx	16
Martin	14	Nymph	14
Ostrich	16	Otter	10
Pelican	8	Porcupine	16
Port Antonio	12	Ranger	8
Rattlesnake	12	Rover	14
Scorpion	16	Shark	16
Star	14	Stork	14
Surprise	16	Swallow	12
Swan	14	Viper	16
Victor	16	Vulture	18
Wasp	8	Wolf	8
Zephir	10		

Armed Ships

Alfred	20	Content	20

Lists

Clytas	20	Greenwich	26
Heart of Oak	20	Lerithe	20
Lioness	26	London	20
Mackworth	20	Merchant	20
Pacific	26	Pricess of Wales	20
Queen	20	Satisfaction	20
Three Brothers	20	Thre Sisters	20
William	20		

Cutters

Alarm	Pusy
Expedition	Ferret
Flying Fish	Folckstone
Griffin	Meredith
Nimble	Pheasant
Rambler	Resolution
Serborne	Sprightly
Tapegeur	True Briton
Wells	

Bombs

Basilisk	Carcass
Etna	Firedrake
Serpent	Terror
Thunder	Vesuvia

Fire Ships

Blast	Comet

Lists

Firebrand
Harpy
Lightning
Salamander
Strombolo
Vulcar

Furnace
Incendiary
Pluto
Spitfire
Sulpher

Royal Yachts

Dorset
Katherine
Media
Royal Charlotte

Tubbs
Mary
Royal Augusta
William and Mary

* * * * * * *

Lists

Pay of Naval Officers

- - - - - - -

<u>The Pay of the Officerx of the Royal Navy in Each</u>
<u>Rate</u>
<u>Flag Officers and the Captains to Flags,</u>
<u>Per Day in Sterling</u>

<u>Rank</u>
Admiral and Commanders-in-Chief
   Of the Fleet
Admiral
Vice-Admiral
Rear-Admiral
1st Captain to the Commander-in-Chief
2nd Captain to the Commander-in-Chief
   and Captain to other Admirals
2nd Captain to Vice-Admirals -
   if first or second rates
2nd Captain to Rear-Admirals -
   have the pay of such rates

* * * * * * *

A Commander-in-Chief is allowed one pound per day for table money.

The Admiral of the Fleet is allowed 50 servants

An Admiral	30
Vice-Admiral	20
Rear-Admiral	15
A Lieutenant, Master, Purser, Surgeon, Chaplain, or Cook	1 for every 60 men

94

Lists

Boatswain, Gunner, ofr Carpenter 2 for every 100
men

* * * * * * *

<u>Staff Officers of the Marines</u>
<u>General</u>
　Forbes
<u>Colonels</u>
　Elliot　　　　　　　Walsingham
　Hotham
<u>Colonels Commandant</u>
　Mackenzie　　　　　Bell
　Smith　　　　　　　Collins
　Carruthers
<u>Lieutenant Colonels</u>
　Mariott　　　　　　Martin
　Brown　　　　　　　Tupper
　Napier　　　　　　　Hughes
　Souter　　　　　　　Trotter
　Innes　　　　　　　　Perkin

Index

Index

Index

BROWNRIFF, 25
BRUCE, 39 Lt Col 1 29 36
BRUMMEL, 39
BUCKLE, 81
BUCKLER, 12
BUDD, 67
BUECKEL, 56
BULLOCK, 28
BUNBURY, 33
BURNET, 19
BURNS, 64
BURROWES, 14
BUSH, 59
BUSKIRK, 71 Lt Col Com 71
BUTLER, 4
BUTTE, 52
BYRON, 81
CAHILL, 18
CAITHNESS, Earl Of 39
CALADINE, 22
CALENDER, 26 62
CALHEART, Maj 25
CALLEN, 64
CALMERS, Lt Col Com 74
CALONER, 4
CALVERT, 21
CAMBIER, 81
CAMERON, 24 27 37-39 42
    64 66 72 75 Angus 38
CAMERONL, Capt 3
CAMMINE, 40
CAMP, 70
CAMPBELL, 9 21-23 25-26 29
    34 37 66-67 69-70 72-73 78
    81 Alex 78 Archibald 38 42
    Archiblad 38 Capt 2-3 Colin
    37-38 Douglas 26 Ducan 42

Duncan 38 F B 10 Hugh 37
    James 37 John 1 Lt Col 30
    37 67 Maj 63 Niel 42
    Robert 37-38 Smollet 38
CAMPELL, Maj Gen 2
CANNING, Lt Col 41
CANNON, 74
CARDEN, 31 Maj 68
CAREY, 17 Col 27
CARFRAE, 41
CARLETON, G 28 Guy 1
CARRIQUE, 16
CARROL, 16
CARRUTHERS, 28 95
CARTER, 9
CARTWRIGHT, 32
CAULFIELD, 28
CAYTON, 17
CHACE, 80
CHALMERS, 80
CHAMPAGNE, 21
CHAPMAN, 21 67 74
CHARLETON, 78 Thomas R
    11 William 11
CHARLTON, 18
CHASE, 80
CHEW, 70
CHEWTON, Lord 1
CHIPMAN, 61
CHISHOLM, 77
CHISHOLME, Colin 38
CHRISTAL, 75
CHRISTIE, 13 25 32
CHURCH, 22
CLAIR, 14 30 32
CLARK, 4 27 40 67
CLARKE, 32 41 80 Lt Col 14

100

Index

101

Index

Index

Index

Index

Index

IMPET, 34
IMRIE, 41
INDSEY, 20
INGLIS, 74 77
INGRAM, 23
INN, 36
INNES, 19 21 23 26-27 37 41
  82 95 Col 75
INNIS, 61
IRVINE, 28
IRVING, 36 Maj 28
IRWINE, Col 30
JACKSON, 17 30 38 72
JACOB, 35
JAGDMEISTER, Dane 44
JAMAISON, 22
JAMES, 33 71 74
JAMIESON, 40
JARVIS, 62
JASLEY, 77
JEFFERSON, 34
JENKINS, 9 70
JESSERYES, 83
JEWELL, 63
JEWETT, 69 71
JOHN, 77
JOHNSNO, 69
JOHNSON, 4 14 22 24 66 Lt
  Col 17
JOHNSTON, 25 64 Thomas 11
  William 11
JOHNSTONE, 36
JONES, 12 14 16 18 20 22-23
  33-34 62 74 76
JONNES, 80
JORDAN, 5
JUNY, 46

JUSTI, 54-55
KAISER, 57
KANE, 64
KAY, 74
KEARNEY, 75
KEATRING, 68
KEENS, 63
KEER, 61
KELLERHAUS, 56
KELLOCK, 62
KELLY, 23 35 76 Gregory 35
KEMPENFELL, 82
KENDRIK, 9
KENNEDY, 27 73-74
KENNEVIE, 41
KENT, 25
KEPPEL, 21 81 Capt 1
KERARSLEY, 32
KERR, 9 13 23 27 30 65
KERSTING, 45
KEYMIS, 15
KIENEN, Jr 53 Sr 53
KIER, 13 79
KIMM, 46
KINCAID, 9
KING, 7 12 63
KINLOCH, 40
KINLOOH, 74
KIRKMAN, 19
KITZEL, Lt Col 55
KLEINSCHMID, 54
KLEINSCHMIDT, 45
KLEINSTEUBER, 54
KLING, 59
KLINGENDER, 46
KLINGSOEHR, 48
KNIES, 55

Index

Index

Index

Index

Index

Index

Index

Index

Index

Index

WILKINSON, 29 33
WILLAIMS, 17
WILLE, 47
WILLET, 76
WILLETT, 66
WILLIAMS, 6 11 76 Capt 3
WILLIAMSON, 36
WILLINGTON, 30 38
WILLIS, 25 70
WILLSON, 37
WILMOT, 72
WILSON, 11-12 62 64 67 69
  79
WINCHESTER, 18
WINLERTON, 25
WINSLOW, 4 61
WIPPLE, 6
WISKER, 52 56
WITTE, 54
WITTY, 28
WOLF, 56

WOLFELEY, 18
WOLPERT, 47
WOOD, 11 15 35 Ens 4
WOOLSEY, 62
WORMLEY, 65
WORMSLEY, 15
WRIGHT, 32 34-35 Jr 10 Maj
  Com 78 Sr 9
WUERFELMANN, 53
WURMB, Maj 50
WYBRANTS, 33
WYLLY, 75
WYNGARD, 23 35 Lt 3
WYVILLA, 25
YELVERTON, 79
YORKE, Lt Col 20
YOUNG, 9 26 67 81
ZIMMERMANN, 51
ZINCK, 46
ZINN, 50
ZOLL, 50

122

THE AUTHOR

Bruce E. Burgoyne was born 25 October 1924 in Benton Harbor, Michigan, and is married with three grown sons. His wife Marie, a Doctor of Education from the University of Southern California, is a helpful research companion and source of encouragement. Mr. Burgoyne's education includes a Master of Arts in Social Science (History, Economics, and Government) from Trinity University in San Antonio, Texas, plus course work at half a dozen other colleges and universities in America and overseas. He has also completed numerous military courses in such subjects as German language, Counterintelligence, and Public Information.

His employment, in addition to recently teaching a seminar course on the Hessians at Delaware State University, has included twenty years of military service in the Navy, Army, and Air Force, and six years as a civilian intelligence officer with the Army. During his military and civilian service he lived six years in Germany during which time he attended German language school in Oberammergau and two months of in-depth study, living in German households and undergoing Berlitz-type training. His daily duties required interviewing and interrogating in German, which further developed his knowledge of the language.

His forty years of research on the role of the Hessians in the American Revolutionary War have taken him and his wife to archives in England and Holland, as well as those in Germany and the United States, and resulted in the translation of more than 35 major Hessian documents.

www.ingramcontent.com/pod-product-compliance
Lightning Source LLC
Chambersburg PA
CBHW060402090426
42734CB00011B/2226